DIPLODOCUS

by Arnold Ringstad

Cody Koala

An Imprint of Pop!
popbooksonline.com

abdobooks.com
Published by Pop!, a division of ABDO, PO Box 398166, Minneapolis, Minnesota 55439. Copyright © 2019 by POP, LLC. International copyrights reserved in all countries. No part of this book may be reproduced in any form without written permission from the publisher. Pop!™ is a trademark and logo of POP, LLC.

Printed in the United States of America, North Mankato, Minnesota

082018
012019

THIS BOOK CONTAINS RECYCLED MATERIALS

Cover Photo: De Agostini Picture Library/Science Source
Interior Photos: De Agostini Picture Library/Science Source, 1; Mark Boulton/Science Source, 5; Mark Hallett Paleoart/Science Source, 6–7; Francois Gohier/Science Source, 9; Shutterstock Images, 10, 14–15, 17 (top); Sam Pierson/Science Source, 12–13; The Natural History Museum, London/Science Source, 17 (bottom left), 17 (bottom right), 18, 20–21

Editor: Meg Gaertner
Series Designer: Laura Mitchell

Library of Congress Control Number: 2018949756
Publisher's Cataloging-in-Publication Data
Names: Ringstad, Arnold, author.
Title: Diplodocus / by Arnold Ringstad.
Description: Minneapolis, Minnesota : Pop!, 2019 | Series: Dinosaurs | Includes online resources and index.
Identifiers: ISBN 9781532161803 (lib. bdg.) | ISBN 9781641855518 (pbk) | ISBN 9781532162862 (ebook)
Subjects: LCSH: Diplodocus--Juvenile literature. | Dinosaurs--Juvenile literature. | Extinct animals--Juvenile literature.
Classification: DDC 567.913--dc23

Hello! My name is

Cody Koala

Pop open this book and you'll find QR codes like this one, loaded with information, so you can learn even more!

Scan this code* and others like it while you read, or visit the website below to make this book pop.

popbooksonline.com/diplodocus

*Scanning QR codes requires a web-enabled smart device with a QR code reader app and a camera.

Table of Contents

Chapter 1

A Gentle Giant

Diplodocus was a tall, long-necked dinosaur. It was longer than two buses put together. It was three times as heavy as an elephant.

Watch a video here!

Diplodocus likely traveled in **herds**. It walked on four even legs.

It stretched its neck high to eat from tall trees. It lowered its head to drink water.

Chapter 2

Leafy Meals

Diplodocus had teeth shaped like pegs. It did not chew its food.

The name Diplodocus is pronounced "di-PLOD-ocus" or "di-plo-DO-cus."

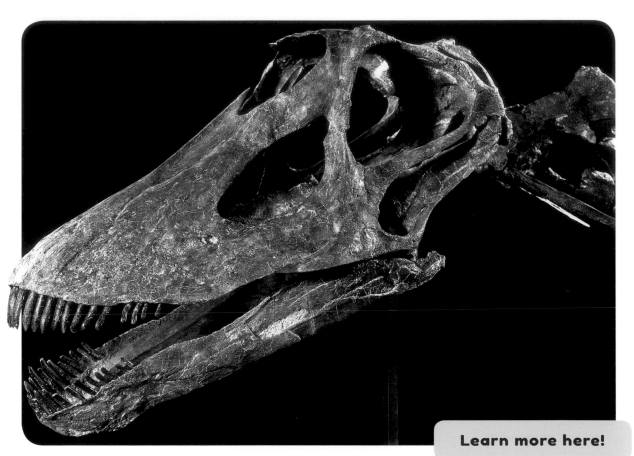

Learn more here!

Instead, the dinosaur stripped leaves from trees. It got a mouthful of plants. Then it swallowed them.

Diplodocus grew new teeth to replace worn down teeth. It got a new tooth every 32 days.

Chapter 3

A Useful Tail

Diplodocus had a long tail. Scientists think it could have been a weapon. Diplodocus could whip **predators** to keep them away.

Learn more here!

Scientists also think their tails helped them reach extra high. They could stand on their back legs.

Their tails would touch the ground. They could **balance** while they ate.

Chapter 4

Diplodocus in Museums

Diplodocus is common in **museums**. Visitors can see it all around the world. One famous Diplodocus is in a museum in England.

Complete an
activity here!

For many years, the **skeleton**'s tail dragged on the ground. This changed in 1993.

Scientists **discovered**
Diplodocus held its tail up.
This helped balance its neck.

The museum raised the tail

to match the new discovery.

Making Connections

Text-to-Self

Would you want to meet a Diplodocus in real life? Why or why not?

Text-to-Text

Have you read any other books about plant-eating dinosaurs? What did you learn?

Text-to-World

Diplodocus had a long neck. What other animals have you seen that have long necks?

Glossary

balance – to stop yourself from tipping over.

discovered – learned something new.

herd – a large group of animals that live and travel together.

museum – a place where people can learn about science and history.

predator – an animal that hunts other animals.

skeleton – the bones that support the body of a human or an animal.

Index

Online Resources

popbooksonline.com

Thanks for reading this Cody Koala book!

Scan this code* and others like it in this book, or visit the website below to make this book pop!

popbooksonline.com/diplodocus

*Scanning QR codes requires a web-enabled smart device with a QR code reader app and a camera.